SIX FIGURE MEETINGS

HOW TO RUN MEETINGS THAT BOOST MORALE AND PROFITS

ANDREW MARTIN

FREILING
AGENCY

Published by Freiling Agency, LLC.

P.O. Box 1264
Warrenton, VA 20188

www.FreilingAgency.com

Paperback ISBN: 978-1-963701-90-6
E-book ISBN: 978-1-963701-01-2

Printed in the United States of America

TABLE OF CONTENTS

Introduction..v

1 The Problem with Meetings............................1

2 Why Do So Many Meetings Go Bad?.............11

3 Have a Point...21

4 Have an Agenda 39

5 Master Meeting Dynamics 51

6 Cultivating Participation 67

7 Facilitating Conflict Resolution....................79

8 Managing Time Effectively...........................91

9 Six Figure Dinners.......................................105

"When conducted efficiently, meetings can be the linchpin that propels teams and organizations toward their goals."

INTRODUCTION

AMIDST THE INCESSANT CALLS, text messages, webinars, notifications, and project management dashboards, Danny Mitchell, a driven and determined manager, found himself ensnared in a relentless cycle of staff meetings that seemed to drag him further away from his goals with each passing day.

Each day as the sun rose and Danny arrived at the office, he navigated through a sea of meetings with coworkers. Staff meeting after staff meeting—that was his life. His schedule was relentless, and today was no different. He sighed heavily, muttering under his breath, "Here we go again."

The first meeting was with the marketing team. Sarah, the head of marketing, seemed to have a penchant for verbosity. She rambled on and on about market trends and customer demographics, while Danny felt his impatience grow with every passing minute. Finally, he couldn't take it anymore and interrupted her with a forced smile, "Sarah, can we get to the point? What's the bottom line here?"

Sarah blinked, taken aback. "Well, Dan, I thought it was important to provide some context..."

He cut her off, irritation bubbling to the surface. "I need solutions, not a history lesson."

The next meeting was with the HR department. Bill, the HR manager, was notorious for his long-winded explanations. He began discussing the company's benefits package, and Danny felt his patience slipping away. He leaned forward, his voice tinged with frustration. "Bill, can you summarize this in three sentences or less?"

Bill stammered, "Well, Daniel, there are several options to consider..."

Danny couldn't contain himself any longer. "I don't have time for details, Bill. Just give me the highlights."

As the day wore on, Daniel's frustration only grew. It was like a never-ending loop of meaningless meetings, each one postponing his real work. He confided in a colleague, Amanda, during a short break. "Amanda, these meetings are a nightmare. I feel like I'm just spinning my wheels."

Amanda nodded in agreement, her expression mirroring his frustration. "I know; we're trapped in a time-sucking vortex."

In the final meeting of the day, Daniel found himself in a room filled with charts and graphs, presented by the finance team. Greg, the head of finance, droned on about budgets and forecasts, while Daniel's mind wandered to the pile of unfinished work on his desk. He slammed his palm on the table, unable to contain his frustration any longer. "Greg, are we on track or not?"

Greg blinked, startled by the outburst. "Well, Daniel, I was just about to get to the…"

Daniel cut him off, his voice firm, "No more details, Greg. Just give me a yes or no."

The meeting ended abruptly, leaving everyone in stunned silence. Danny stormed out of the room, his frustration boiling over.

As he headed back to his office, he couldn't help but wonder if there was a way to break free from this never-ending cycle of aimless meetings that seemed to be leading him nowhere. In the fast-paced world of business, time was money, and he couldn't afford to waste any more of it on meetings that felt like a futile exercise in futility.

Does this story sound familiar?

When you ask people how they feel about attending and participating in meetings, the response is often a unanimous and resounding "NO THANKS!" Meetings are widely regarded as a source of frustration and inconvenience, both in the workplace and in other various non-work-related settings. People complain that they find themselves trapped in too many meetings, and for too long. Meetings, it seems, have earned a notorious reputation.

People say meetings are a hindrance to productivity and an obstacle to achieving success. They are frequently viewed as time-consuming affairs that divert people from their core tasks, leaving them with a sense of wasted time and unfulfilled goals and objectives. Even in non-work scenarios, such as community gatherings or social events, people lament the seemingly endless discussions and deliberations that often leave them feeling drained and unproductive.

The Office, a popular TV show, hilariously pokes fun at corporate culture by brilliantly satirizing the mundane and often absurd aspects of staff meetings. Through its quirky characters, awkward interactions, and mockumentary-style filming, the series highlights the pointlessness of endless meetings and the absurdity of corporate jargon. From the overzealous boss Michael Scott's bizarre meeting themes to Dwight Schrute's eccentric role-playing exercises, the show cleverly exaggerates the awkwardness and inefficiency of office gatherings, offering a comical and relatable perspective on the everyday drudgery of corporate life. Why do we find it so funny? Because it's all too true.

How about you—do you despise meetings?

As for myself, I proudly consider myself a meeting contrarian. Unlike most people, I love meetings.

However, let me clarify that my affinity is not for just *any* meeting; it's for well-managed, purposeful meetings that serve as a catalyst for accomplishing tasks and achieving goals. My colleagues jokingly refer to me as the "meeting whisperer," because I seem to have a keen sense for how to make them work. And in all seriousness, meetings are not just a part of my routine; they are my passion and expertise. Meetings—effective meetings—are how I get more out of people and the organizations I manage.

I firmly believe that when handled correctly, meetings can be a powerful tool for driving progress, fostering collaboration, and bringing about positive change. They offer a unique platform for individuals to come together, share insights, exchange ideas, and collectively strategize for success. When conducted efficiently, meetings can be the linchpin that propels teams and organizations toward their goals.

My conviction in the powerful potential of meetings is so strong that I founded a company around the concept. At Six Figure Dinners, we've devised an innovative way for entrepreneurs to meet together regularly and discuss not just their wins and losses, but also the challenges they face in their businesses. This approach transforms traditional, aimless meetings into dynamic, results-oriented sessions where real problems are solved and actionable strategies are developed. While this book is not about my company specifically (although I'll share about it in the last chapter), it is about how to master the art of impactful meetings.

I call them "six figure meetings" because they get the most of your people and your profits. A six figure meeting will optimize your organization and propel it toward growth and success. In short, it will make you more money and reduce your stress levels while you're at it.

While hosting and managing meetings might not be everyone's cup of tea, I firmly believe that with the right approach, anyone can turn every meeting into a driving force behind personal and professional advancement. So, while the prevailing sentiment may be a resounding "NO" when it comes to meetings, I want to change your mind. That's why I wrote this book. This book is for people who lead meetings and for those who attend them, which is pretty much all of us. By learning to adopt best practices in meeting management, setting clear objectives, and fostering a culture of respect for participants' time and contributions, you can work toward making meetings a more positive and constructive part of your professional and personal life.

I promise not to mince words or waste your time with this book. We're all busy in our businesses and our lives, so my intention is to offer you an easy-to-digest primer on how to host and manage better meetings. My desire is that this book will actually mimic a successful meeting. It will get to the point, share essential information, get you thinking constructively, and provide you with a positive outcome. Inside the pages of this book, we'll look at six distinct ways you can master the art of impactful meetings:

- Have a point going into your meetings.
- Create and distribute a meeting agenda.
- Learn how to master meeting dynamics.
- Cultivate participation among participants.
- Facilitate better conflict resolution.
- Manage your time more effectively.

We all want our meetings to solve problems, generate better ideas, and increase our revenue and profit. After reading this book, I believe you can learn to love meetings, just as I do, because when well-managed, they will get you closer to your goals.

Let me help you say "YES!" to meetings.

"A minute of planning is
worth an hour of execution,
but we don't even take
a minute to plan most
of our meetings."

1

THE PROBLEM WITH MEETINGS

MARK CUBAN, THE SERIAL investor and shark on the popular TV program *Shark Tank*, once told *Inc.* magazine that meetings are a complete waste of time. "The only way you're going to get me for a meeting is if you're writing me a check," he said. Likewise, billionaire and Tesla founder Elon Musk also urges his employees to forgo meetings, calling them a "blight" on companies.

I think it's safe to say that we all have problems with most of the meetings we participate in. It doesn't take a billionaire to see the problem.

Not every meeting is a bad idea, though, and I definitely won't go as far as Mark Cuban, who believes that meetings are worthless. On the contrary, I believe meetings can be an integral and powerful part of moving organizations forward. But time is money. As a leader or manager, you know this instinctively, and you probably do your best to manage your time effectively. Yet you probably don't think much about how to take control of the time you waste in meetings. Why not? The problem begins with the fact that we're not educated or trained on how to manage our meetings.

Nobody Teaches You How to Run a Good Meeting

Imagine yourself as a dedicated MBA student embarking on a transformative journey at the prestigious Wharton School of Business, renowned as one of the foremost business schools in the United States. As you step onto this hallowed academic ground, you enter into an immersive and intellectually stimulating environment designed to equip you with the knowledge and skills necessary for success in the complex world of business.

At Wharton, the core curriculum is not just any curriculum; it's an intensive, cross-functional powerhouse that lays the foundation for your future as a business leader. The comprehensive program delves deep into the essential building blocks of business, instilling in you the fundamentals of leadership, effective communication, and analytical prowess. Throughout your academic journey, you'd immerse yourself in a diverse array of subjects, each carefully selected to arm you with the tools you need to excel in the corporate landscape.

You'd grapple with the intricacies of marketing and management, unravel the mysteries of microeconomics, harness the power of statistics and regression analysis, decode the language of accounting, explore the intricacies of human resource management, and confront the complex world of business ethics. With each subject, you'd be guided by some of the most respected and accomplished business professors in the country, individuals who bring a wealth of knowledge and practical experience to the classroom. However, there'd be one noticeable gap in this comprehensive education: The absence of any coursework dedicated to the art and science of hosting effective meetings.

Surprisingly, "managing meetings" remains conspicuously absent from the college curriculum; apparently, the thought of teaching about it does not even cross the minds of Wharton's professors. It is a notable omission in an otherwise robust and forward-thinking educational program. I've looked and I can't find a single MBA program in America that offers coursework on meeting management (and I've looked high and low!). The result is a landscape where future business leaders graduate with a wealth of knowledge but lack the essential skills to effectively navigate the dynamic world of meetings.

It's ironic that business school graduates have to "wing it" when they host meetings, as they will spend a great deal of time attending and leading them. Think about it: When you arrive at the office on Monday morning and look at your calendar for the week, it appears that you'll be spending nearly half of your working hours meeting with colleagues. There are one-on-one meetings, meetings with direct reports, team meetings, check-ins, decision-making meetings, finance meetings, project management meetings, company-wide meetings, meetings with human resources, and the list goes on. It's hard to imagine a workday that doesn't include meetings. Yet the topic was (and is) virtually ignored during our formal education. I think this is particularly ironic since business school is simply a series of meetings!

Work Revolves around Meetings

Have you ever taken a moment to consider how many meetings you participate in on a weekly basis? According to the insights provided by Fellow, a company dedicated to enhancing team meetings through collaborative tools and resources, businesses in the United States convene an astonishing 55 million meetings every single week. That's a monumental figure!

Typical employees participate in five to ten meetings per week. That's a lot of meetings. The pressure is even more pronounced for executives and managers, who often need to juggle, on average, more than a dozen weekly meetings in their schedules. When you break down the time allocation, it's obvious that we all spend a significant portion of our workdays engrossed in meetings. On average, we devote one-third to one-half of our total work hours to these gatherings. It's a substantial investment of our professional time, emphasizing the need for meetings to be more meaningful and productive.

As you examine your own weekly calendar, you might notice that Mondays tend to be the peak day for meetings. Perhaps it's the eagerness to kick-start the week with discussions and planning that drives this trend. However, the statistics take an interesting turn when you look at meeting duration. Wednesdays emerge as the day when meetings tend to stretch on the longest. It's a midweek challenge familiar to many professionals as they navigate through prolonged discussions and decisions. The average meeting lasts over an hour, and when you multiply that by the number of meetings in a typical week, the cumulative time spent becomes staggering.

It's ironic that the reason we have meetings is to grow our organizations and make them more profitable. In essence, meetings are meant to be instrumental in driving the financial success of the companies. However, the unfortunate reality is that we often squander our most invaluable resource—time—in unproductive and inefficient meetings. We actually end up incurring substantial losses due to poor meeting practices. Rather than help our top and bottom lines, the meetings end up hurting.

Meetings Drive Down Revenue and Profits

To put the cost of unproductive meetings into perspective, consider the staggering figure of over $37 billion in annual losses attributed to these counterproductive gatherings. This staggering sum underscores the magnitude of the issue at hand.

Let's break down these costs further for a clearer understanding. Imagine you have a team of ten meeting participants, each with an average annual salary of $70,000. If this group convenes twice a week, with each meeting lasting an hour, the cumulative cost to the company amounts to a staggering $35,000 per year. In simpler terms, each of these meetings carries a hefty price tag of $337. This financial expenditure is not just about dollars and cents; it also represents a significant allocation of employee working hours. In fact, these meetings consume a total of 1,040 employee working hours annually.

Now, let's take it a step further and consider the opportunity cost involved. Picture a scenario in which a manager holds a two-hour meeting with eighteen colleagues to make critical decisions. In this situation, they are essentially spending person-hours equivalent to one employee's entire week of work. This vividly illustrates the hidden costs associated with unproductive meetings—the hours spent in meetings could have been channeled into meaningful, value-generating tasks.

These numbers serve as a stark reminder of the high price we pay when meetings fail to fulfill their intended purpose. The financial implications are significant, but it's also crucial to recognize the intangible costs, such as reduced employee morale, decreased productivity, and missed growth opportunities. It becomes evident that addressing the issue of bad meetings is not just a matter of convenience; it's a strategic imperative for any organization striving to optimize its resources and achieve financial success.

A good accountant will penny-pinch everything from travel expenses to office supply expenses, yet will not account for all the time wasted in meetings. Bad meetings never make their way onto financial statements. They are truly a hidden cost with no built-in accountability or assessments. Nobody in an organization is ever tasked with "owning" the meetings. There is no chief meeting officer, and nobody asks the question, "How can we do our meetings better?" We all simply take it for granted that bad meetings are a part of the workday. We put up with them, we complain about them, but we rarely plan to make them better. A minute of planning is worth an hour of execution, but we don't even take a minute to plan most of our meetings.

Apparently, I'm not the only one who believes that poorly managed meetings are a drain on revenue and profit. Shopify, the world's biggest ecommerce platform, also decided to combat this phenomenon. It was the announcement heard round the internet: Shopify was doing away with most meetings. In a January 2023 memo, the e-commerce platform called it "useful subtraction," a way to free up time to allow people to get stuff done. "We deleted 322,000 hours of meetings," Shopify's Chief Operating Officer Kaz Nejatian proudly shared in a recent interview. Naturally, as a tech company, Shopify wrote code to do this. A bot went into everyone's calendars and purged all recurring meetings with three or more people, giving them that time back. "Those hours were the equivalent of adding 150 new employees," Nejatian said. I'm not convinced it's a good idea to literally purge our calendars of meetings. That feels too abrupt.

Salesforce also recently announced a less sudden change to meetings and productivity. The company implemented a "week without meetings" in an attempt to combat meeting fatigue and the exhaustion caused by the need to be available all day and participate in numerous meetings. As a result of the experiment, 93 percent of the employees reported at least one positive aspect of a week without meetings, 61 percent said they worked the same number of hours, 20 percent said they worked fewer hours, and about half of the people said they learned how to work better asynchronously. In parallel with Salesforce's experiment, Citigroup, the global bank, also decided to make changes to work meetings. For example, they decided to shorten meetings to 50 minutes to give all employees a ten-minute break.

These seem to be more reasonable approaches to saving money and increasing profits. At the very least, they draw attention to a problem that is largely ignored. Good meeting management is, unfortunately, ignored in most companies and organizations. We simply don't take the time to understand the value of good meetings and what we can do to overcome the barriers to change that.

"I believe groups can, in most cases, make better decisions than individuals can on their own."

2

WHY DO SO MANY MEETINGS GO BAD?

MEETINGS OFTEN BECOME A cesspool of chaos, indecision, confusion, and frustration. We'll take a deep dive into all the reasons later in this book, but for now, suffice it to say that in most business settings, good decisions are not often made in meetings or as the result of them, but rather by individuals who are working alone. When you're sitting in a meeting, do you often privately acknowledge to yourself: "I could do this better on my own rather than sitting through this meeting"? I bet you do, and in fact, you probably could. Why do individuals feel that they make better decisions than groups do? I believe there are two paramount reasons why "groupthink" is a pervasive problem in our workplaces.

The phenomenon of groupthink isn't my own. It was first coined by Yale University social psychologist Irving Janis in 1972, and it shed light on one of the underlying reasons behind the often less-than-ideal outcomes of meetings. Janis's theory posits that gatherings of even the most intelligent individuals often lead to suboptimal decisions. It seems counterintuitive, but group interactions, and the psychological pressures that individuals face within these settings, often unexpectedly result in poor decisions.

In his best-selling book, *Groupthink: Psychological Studies of Policy Decisions and Fiascoes*, Janis uses the poor decision-making process during the Bay of Pigs crisis of John F. Kennedy's presidency as an example. Kennedy's advisors, all smart and experienced, formed a tight-knit group, but it lacked diversity in opinions and became susceptible to a narrow perspective. They were known for their loyalty to the president and shared objectives, but they exhibited overconfidence in the plan's success. They believed that the operation would be swift and would be met with little resistance. Members of the group downplayed potential risks and shortcomings of the plan, convincing themselves that it was foolproof. Dissenting voices during their meetings, such as those who questioned the feasibility of the operation, were often silenced or marginalized. This suppression of dissenting opinions contributed to a lack of critical examination of the plan. The group maintained an illusion of unanimity, with members hesitating to voice doubts or concerns. This false consensus further reinforced their flawed decisions during their long late-night meetings.

What was the result? The Bay of Pigs invasion turned into a disaster. Cuban forces, with support from the Soviet Union, easily repelled the U.S.-backed invasion, leading to the capture and imprisonment of over a thousand Cuban exiles. It not only tarnished the reputation of the United States but also escalated tensions between the superpowers during the Cold War.

It was a poignant example of how poorly managed meetings can have dire consequences in high-stakes decision-making processes.

The Problem with Groupthink

Janis suggested that in the pursuit of consensus thinking during meetings, we inadvertently overlook potential problems or dissenting viewpoints. We tend to "go along to get along." This desire for harmony and unity often leads to conformity of thought, where dissenters may feel pressured to align with the prevailing consensus, stifling critical thinking and diverse perspectives. I think we've all experienced meetings where we corporately, yet privately, agree to get behind an idea simply to get the meeting over with or to appear supportive of the organization and its goals.

This deficiency in diverse perspectives can lead to a multitude of problems, primarily stemming from the fact that no single meeting participant possesses all the relevant information. Consequently, decisions made in such meetings tend to occur in a vacuum, devoid of the more holistic and informed insights that are essential for effective decision-making. In essence, meetings often become breeding grounds for guesswork, either due to the presence of the wrong individuals at the table or an environment that fails to foster constructive discussion. The result is a significant loss of efficiency and effectiveness in decision-making processes during meetings.

This knowledge gap results in less-informed choices and suboptimal outcomes. In a business context, the consequences of groupthink can be particularly detrimental. Employees and managers may become so focused on consensus that they neglect to critically evaluate potential issues or alternative approaches. The fear of disrupting the status quo or going against the grain can lead to self-censorship, inhibiting the free exchange of ideas and innovative thinking. As a result, meetings can become breeding grounds for excessive optimism, where participants collectively ignore any suggestion of negative consequences because they are convinced of the infallibility of their ideas.

In essence, what this highlights is that effective meetings do not simply occur by chance. Left to their own devices, meetings easily fall prey to the insidious grip of groupthink, resulting in frustration and subpar decisions. I once heard it said that "a committee is a group of people who individually can do nothing, but who, as a group, can meet and decide that nothing can be done." Indeed, while this sentiment may hold true in many cases, it doesn't have to be this way. When people come together collaboratively and cooperatively, meetings can have the potential to yield the best decisions.

I believe groups can, in most cases, make better decisions than individuals can on their own.

After all, wisdom is often gained through conversation and the exchange of ideas. However, the key lies in ensuring that these conversations are not only productive but also open to dissenting voices and critical thinking. Meetings themselves are not inherently problematic; it's the manner in which they are conducted that can make all the difference. Therefore, the focus should not be on whether or not to have meetings but rather on how to conduct them effectively, fostering an environment that encourages diversity of thought and leads to the best possible outcomes. But before we unpack all the answers, there's another reason meetings often disappoint us.

Meetings Make Us Mad

Another significant challenge associated with bad meetings is their potential to put people in a negative mood, which can have a cascading impact on both individual and organizational levels. Understanding this psychological aspect sheds light on why addressing meeting effectiveness is not just about improving processes but also about fostering a more positive and productive work environment.

Bad meetings often elicit emotions and reactions in people that are akin to experiencing an interruption in their workflow, and interruptions are typically perceived as negative events. When you're in the midst of your work, focused on tasks, and are suddenly called to attend a meeting, it disrupts your rhythm and takes you away from what you were engaged in. This abrupt shift in focus can be jarring and unwelcome, and it can put you in a state of discomfort, irritability, or even resistance.

The negative impact of this disruption isn't confined to just one person. It's a shared experience among all meeting participants. When everyone in a meeting is subjected to the same sense of interruption and distraction, the collective mood can quickly turn sour. The negativity spreads, creating an atmosphere of frustration and impatience that can hinder effective communication and collaboration. Furthermore, when people find themselves in negative mood states, they tend to become less open-minded and creative. This is a critical point to consider, as creativity and innovative thinking are often essential for problem-solving and decision-making in meetings. When individuals are mentally closed off due to their negative emotional state, it becomes challenging to generate new ideas, explore alternative solutions, and arrive at optimal decisions. Consequently, organizations suffer not only in terms of wasted time but also in missed opportunities for innovation and growth.

Time Is Your Most Valuable Resource

My message is plain and simple: It's time to plan good meetings. A group of people truly can be smarter and more effective than one single individual. None of us is "good" enough to do it all alone. We need each other, and we need group settings. I think we all acknowledge that, but the problem is that we don't take time to make it happen.

Time is the most valuable thing you have going for you, right? We're all pressed for time, both at home and at work. Not a day goes by when we don't think to ourselves, "If only I had more time." And when asked how things are going, we often find ourselves answering, "Things are going great, but I'm really busy!"

Time is indeed a universal equalizer, given in equal measure to every individual in increments of twenty-four hours a day. In a world bustling with endless distractions and obligations, it is crucial to recognize and embrace the notion that time is our most precious asset. It's also non-renewable and cannot be bought or negotiated. Understanding the irrevocable nature of time compels us to value it and use it wisely. Think about this in the context of your next meeting. And remember, speed is not the sole metric of productivity, and success does not necessitate constant haste. By embracing intentional meeting planning and a more mindful approach to meetings, you can unlock your full potential, make the most of your valuable time, and set the stage for even greater accomplishments in both your personal and professional life.

Stop running so fast. Govern yourself, and think ahead more. Be intentional. We live in a fast and furious world, but you truly can slow down the pace without sacrificing your success. Nowhere is speed a productivity metric. So I encourage you to take more time to plan, especially in reference to your meetings. If you could reduce time spent in meetings by 50 percent and increase the effectiveness of your meetings by 50 percent, you'd have a 100 percent turnaround! I've seen it done. In fact, this is what I do, and I believe you can do the same.

In the next chapter, I'll share some practical, tactical ways to improve the meetings you attend and those you manage. These strategies can be transformative, but their true value becomes evident when you embrace a fundamental shift in your approach to time. It all begins with recognizing the importance of taking your time seriously. In a world that often glorifies speed and multitasking, it's easy to find ourselves constantly rushing from one task to another. However, it's crucial to remind ourselves that not all endeavors benefit from this breakneck pace. The art of slowing down and governing oneself is not a concession of success; rather, it's a strategy for achieving even greater success.

By implementing these strategies and shifting your perspective on time management, you can begin to experience the profound benefits of more efficient meetings. Imagine the impact of reducing the time spent in meetings by half while simultaneously doubling their effectiveness—it results in a remarkable 100 percent turnaround. I can personally attest to witnessing such transformations, and I firmly believe that you have the capacity to achieve the same level of success.

"If almost every meeting you host feels aimless, you truly have nobody to blame but yourself."

3

HAVE A POINT

HERE'S THE MOST IRONIC thing about meetings. When I engage in conversations with CEOs and other leaders who conduct meetings, a common and intriguing pattern consistently emerges. These "high-ranking" leaders, who are often at the helm of their organizations, express a significant level of dissatisfaction with the outcomes of *their own meetings*. What's particularly striking is that this dissatisfaction often appears to be as intense, if not more so, than what is expressed by the participants of these meetings. That's right: they seem oddly aware that their meetings aren't going well. Yet what is equally perplexing is their apparent resistance to change, as they continue to adhere to the same meeting practices, seemingly oblivious to the need for different strategy.

Why do so many accomplished leaders willingly endure the considerable strain that meetings place on their time and mental well-being? Their responses typically revolve around a common theme: the perception of meetings as a "necessary evil." Sometimes this viewpoint is passionately defended, emphasizing the belief that meetings are an indispensable aspect of their leadership role. In essence, they view themselves as dutiful soldiers, willingly marching into what they acknowledge to be unproductive meetings, all in the name of what they perceive as best for the business. They simply put up with it.

This paradox is both fascinating and telling. On one hand, leaders clearly recognize the dissatisfaction and inefficiencies inherent in their meetings. They are not blind to the fact that the status quo is far from ideal. However, on the other hand, they feel beholden to conventional practices and organizational expectations. There's a palpable pressure to conform, and a fear of disrupting established routines often prevails. The prevailing belief that meetings, even when poorly managed, are an essential and irreplaceable component of business operations perpetuates a seemingly endless cycle of frustration and inefficiency.

This paradox raises several important questions. Why do leaders, who are in a unique position to effect change, choose to remain entrenched in practices that undermine their productivity and that of their organizations? What drives this pervasive belief in the necessity of meetings, even when their detrimental effects are acknowledged? And, most importantly, how can these leaders be empowered to break free from this cycle and embark on a path toward more effective and purposeful meetings?

The First Step toward Better Meetings

Addressing these questions is a critical step toward transforming the meeting culture within organizations led by these CEOs and leaders. It involves challenging deeply ingrained assumptions, fostering a culture of continuous improvement, and providing the necessary tools and strategies to enable leaders to reclaim their time, enhance productivity, and achieve meaningful results from their meetings. By recognizing the paradox and the potential for change, organizations can unlock new possibilities for more efficient and impactful meetings at all levels of leadership.

I shared in the last chapter how time is zero-sum. Once it's wasted, time is gone forever. Every minute spent in a wasteful meeting eats into time for solo work that's equally essential. It's eating into both the top-line and bottom-line of every business. The irony is that the point of most meetings is to somehow increase the top and bottom line, at least in theory, but in reality, most meetings don't have a point at all. A change in strategy is crucial.

In this chapter, I'll share with you my advice to every leader about the first and foremost action to take before and during every meeting they lead: Have a point. You might be surprised at how easy it is to begin to turn things around when you've established and communicated the "point" of your meetings! It seems too simple, right?

It is an undeniable fact that a significant portion of all meetings lacks a clear point or purpose. Meetings often commence without any definitive objective in mind and conclude without achieving any meaningful outcome. The absence of a clear point in a meeting sets the stage for a range of negative consequences, which can significantly hinder productivity and squander valuable time and resources. When have you walked into a meeting where the leader began by explaining the point of the meeting?

The unfortunate reality is that a significant number of meetings begin on a less-than-ideal note, marked by confusion and a lack of clarity. It's not uncommon for participants to gather in a conference room without a clear understanding of the meeting's purpose, agenda, or expected outcomes. This initial ambiguity can lead to a sense of frustration and disengagement among those in attendance. As the meeting kicks off, attendees may find themselves grasping for context or struggling to discern the relevance of the discussions. In such situations, valuable time is wasted, and the meeting's potential for fostering productive collaboration is compromised. Addressing this issue and ensuring that meetings commence with a clear and concise purpose is pivotal to transforming them from sources of confusion into forums for effective communication and decision-making.

One of the primary ramifications of a meeting without a point is *aimlessness*. Without a defined purpose or objective, discussions within the meeting tend to meander, lacking focus and direction. Participants may engage in tangential conversations or explore unrelated topics, leading to a significant loss of productivity. The absence of a clear point leaves attendees unsure about the purpose of the meeting and the desired outcomes, contributing to a sense of confusion and frustration. During an aimless meeting, participants often find themselves engaged in discussions that lack structure, relevance, and a clear objective. They may engage in idle chit-chat, unrelated anecdotes, or meandering conversations that stray away from the intended purpose, if one was defined at all. At the end, the lack of a clear point leaves attendees unsure of what they are expected to achieve or contribute to the meeting.

If almost every meeting you host feels aimless, you truly have nobody to blame but yourself. If you haven't provided some concrete direction, everyone else in the meeting will make up a competing direction. When topics are introduced haphazardly or without a logical progression, making it challenging for participants to follow the discussion, the outcome will likely place you in a worse position than when the meeting started. Chaos results in chaos, all because you didn't have a point in the first place. Or maybe you had a point but were unable to communicate it effectively.

Fortunately, there are some simple fixes to ensure that you and everyone else in the room will understand the "point" to your meeting. Defining the purpose and objectives of a meeting is a fundamental step toward ensuring its effectiveness and productivity. As the host, your ability to communicate these elements clearly and concisely to participants is crucial for steering the meeting in the right direction.

Why We Forget to Make a Point

Several excuses are often used by leaders who fail to adequately explain the point of a meeting. You might fall victim to one or all of them. These excuses can manifest individually or collectively, leaving even the most well-intentioned leaders vulnerable to these pitfalls.

Some leaders assume that the purpose of the meeting is self-evident or known to everyone, leading them to skip the introduction. They are often overly familiar with the subject matter, so they may not see the need to explain the point. However, what is apparent to the leader may not be so for all participants. This is true of almost all communication in life, but it is especially a problem during meetings. When you prioritize content over context, you mistakenly assume that the former will drive the meeting's success. The problem with this ambiguity is that when people don't understand the point of the meeting, it will likely run off course, frustrating everyone in the room.

Another significant obstacle that leaders often grapple with is the apprehension that explaining the point of a meeting might lead to resistance or disagreement from participants. This fear can cast a long shadow over the decision to be upfront about the meeting's objectives. Leaders, driven by a desire for a harmonious and smooth meeting, may hesitate to communicate the purpose with absolute clarity. They might worry that by explicitly outlining their objectives, they could potentially invite pushback, opposition, or even conflict. This apprehension stems from a well-intentioned but sometimes misguided aspiration to maintain a veneer of agreement and avoid confrontational or uncomfortable interactions within the group.

However, this fear-based approach is fraught with risks. By sidestepping the disclosure of the meeting's true purpose, leaders inadvertently sow the seeds of confusion. Participants, left in the dark about the meeting's objectives, will form their own assumptions or interpretations, which can vary widely. This divergence in understanding can result in disjointed discussions, a lack of consensus, and ultimately, a meeting that fails to achieve its intended outcomes. Moreover, the fear of resistance or disagreement can undermine the very essence of productive meetings. Constructive dissent and diverse viewpoints are often catalysts for innovation and sound decision-making. By stifling these critical elements, leaders unintentionally hinder the potential for robust discussion and exploration of different perspectives.

How to Make Your Point

Don't let the people in your meeting create their own context. As a meeting leader, you need to succinctly address the context. Leaders who recognize the significance of setting the context and articulating the point of a meeting are more likely to create a more productive, engaged, and successful gathering. It's essential to provide meeting participants with a comprehensive understanding of the broader context in which the meeting is taking place.

Let me be clear: Making a point doesn't need to be a complex or time-consuming affair. In fact, you're better off to keep it simple. At the very minimum, you should begin each meeting with at least a brief statement of why everyone is in the room. If you simply do that, and nothing more, you'll come out yards ahead of where you are now. For example, you might start a meeting this way:

Thank you all for joining me today. I want to be crystal clear about the purpose of this meeting. We are here to discuss the imminent threat posed by our competitor's new product. Our objective today is to begin to formulate a strategic response so we can start the process of introducing a similar product. There is no room for ambiguity or hesitation, so let's all be focused and clear with our words.

Again, it's important to be brief, clear, and leave no room for ambiguity. A good meeting leader can take also things a little further by:

- Ensuring that the group is aware of the overarching objectives and strategic goals of the organization. This context helps participants understand how their contributions in the meeting align with the broader mission of the company.
- Sharing basic information about ongoing projects, initiatives, or key activities within the organization. Participants should grasp how the meeting relates to these efforts and why their involvement is essential.
- Identifying any pressing challenges or opportunities that will be addressed in the meeting. By highlighting these issues, participants can appreciate the significance of their discussions and contributions in relation to solving real-world problems or capitalizing on opportunities.

Effectively conveying this context empowers participants with the knowledge they need to engage meaningfully in the meeting. It underscores the importance of their input and reinforces the connection between the meeting's purpose and the broader organizational landscape. When you give context, you reframe everyone's thinking toward your desired goals. When you do this, you now have a point for your meeting and a clear reason for being there.

Identify the Desired Outcome

Moving beyond "point" and context, it will also help to pinpoint the outcome or results you aspire to achieve by the end of the meeting. You want all participants to understand not only why they are there, but also *what will happen when they leave the room.* Remember not every meeting is created equal, nor should it aim for the same outcome. So a meeting's success hinges on the clarity of its objectives, and these objectives might be expressed in clear, actionable terms:

- **Decision-making:** Some meetings are convened with the primary aim of making decisions that are critical to the organization's progress. In such cases, it is paramount to clearly state what those decisions entail. Specify the nature of each decision, its scope, and why it is of utmost importance. By providing a clear decision-making agenda, participants can come prepared to contribute meaningfully to the process, ensuring that the outcome aligns with the organization's goals.

- **Idea generation:** Innovation is the lifeblood of businesses seeking to thrive in today's competitive landscape. Meetings designed to foster idea generation should be meticulously planned. Specify the types of ideas or solutions you're looking for. Whether it's brainstorming new product concepts, refining marketing strategies, or tackling operational challenges, participants should know precisely what is expected of them. This clarity empowers creative thinking and drives the generation of actionable ideas that can propel the organization forward.
- **Feedback gathering:** Collecting feedback is an essential aspect of any business operation, from product development to employee performance evaluations. When the objective of a meeting is to gather feedback, outline the specific areas or topics on which feedback is sought. Be explicit about the feedback's purpose and how it will be used. This ensures that participants focus their contributions on the designated areas, resulting in more constructive and targeted feedback.
- **Information sharing:** In a rapidly evolving business environment, the efficient sharing of information is paramount. Meetings convened

primarily for information sharing should leave no room for ambiguity. Indicate what information will be shared and its relevance to the participants, ensuring that the content is presented in a structured and coherent manner. This not only keeps participants informed but also underscores the importance of the information being conveyed.

By categorizing meetings based on their intended outcomes and expressing them in precise terms, organizations can optimize the effectiveness of their gatherings. Clear objectives empower participants to prepare adequately, engage meaningfully, and contribute purposefully, ultimately leading to more productive meetings and tangible outcomes that drive business success.

Defining the desired outcome provides participants with a concrete sense of purpose. It offers clarity about what needs to be accomplished during the meeting and helps everyone stay on track toward achieving that goal. People tend to be more patient when they know the end result will be positive. You might be surprised at how much longer they're willing to remain engaged during the meeting if it's going to solve their problems. It's not meetings themselves that frustrate people; it's how they don't solve their problems. If meetings solved more of their problems, then they'd happily attend and engage in them.

Again, have a point to your meeting. Clarify your purpose and desired outcomes. How many meetings have you attended where the leader communicated any of this? My guess is not very many, and possibly none. This is why meetings are often so aimless. But if you take some time to establish context, outcome, and objectives, you're guaranteed a less frustrating and more productive meeting. Don't let this intimidate you. It doesn't have to be perfect. In fact, any of what I just shared will probably be more than what you're already doing.

Recognize Why Meeting Participants Have Been Invited

I also believe one of the primary problems with most meetings is that participants often don't understand why they are even in the room. As a leader, part of your job is to carefully select each participant for each meeting you host. It's a perplexing scenario where individuals, often talented and capable, gather around the conference table or assemble in virtual meeting spaces, yet each person's purpose remains shrouded in ambiguity. This fog of uncertainty that envelops meeting participants is a poignant illustration of a fundamental issue: the lack of clarity in assembling the right individuals for a particular meeting. You can't "have a point" if you don't have the right people in the room in the first place.

As a leader within an organization, a significant aspect of your role is the art of discernment, the skillful curation of meeting attendees. Your task transcends merely orchestrating meetings; it extends to crafting a selected ensemble of participants for each specific gathering. Choosing participants isn't a perfunctory exercise but rather a strategic act that demands some thoughtfulness and precision. It hinges on your ability to answer the fundamental question: "Who needs to be in the room, and why?" This question serves as the cornerstone of productive meetings. It entails an in-depth understanding of the meeting's objectives, the expertise required, and the potential contributions each participant can make.

I can't speak directly to how you should select and vet your meeting participants. Every organization is unique. Some are small; some are large. Some meetings need just a few people while others might need dozens. But my point is that attendees need to know why they're in the meeting.

At the outset of every meeting, recognize everyone's specific role, and briefly describe why they've all been invited. In the next chapter, we'll discuss who to invite to meetings and why, but for now let's focus on the importance of introducing the participants in a way that will shed more light on the meeting's purpose. Incidentally, I find that this essential step is skipped in almost every meeting. The leader usually dives in and assumes all attendees understand why they are there and why everyone else is there. Wrong! If you don't know why you've been invited, what's the point of being there?

It's absolutely crucial to acknowledge and recognize the specific role of each participant in the room at the beginning of every meeting. By briefly describing why individuals have been invited, the leader can provide valuable context that sheds light on the meeting's purpose. While a detailed exploration of who should be invited to a meeting, and why, will be discussed in the next chapter, it is essential here to highlight the significance of introducing participants as a means to clarify the meeting's point.

When you define who's there and why, it sets the stage for effective collaboration and engagement. By explicitly acknowledging each participant's expertise, knowledge, and unique contributions, the meeting leader creates an atmosphere that fosters respect, inclusivity, and collaboration. This recognition allows participants to understand the value they bring to the meeting and instills a sense of purpose in their contributions.

Introducing participants also provides essential context for the meeting's objectives. By briefly describing why individuals have been invited, the meeting leader highlights the relevance and significance of their presence. This contextual information helps participants understand how their specific expertise or perspective contributes to the meeting's goals and objectives. It also facilitates a shared understanding among attendees, ensuring that everyone is aligned with the purpose and direction of the discussions.

Furthermore, introducing participants can enhance communication and encourage active participation. When attendees are aware of their roles and backgrounds, they are more likely to engage in meaningful dialogue, ask relevant questions, and offer valuable insights. This familiarity reduces the barriers to effective communication and encourages a collaborative environment where diverse perspectives can be shared and considered.

By explicitly recognizing why individuals have been invited, the meeting leader acknowledges the value they bring to the table. This recognition fosters a sense of inclusion among participants, reinforcing their commitment to actively contribute to the meeting.

In the next chapter, we will delve deeper into the topic of intentionality during your meetings by having an agenda. But before you can create an agenda, you need a clear point or purpose. When you arrive at work and sit down at your desk, you try to establish a point to your day. You try to identify the tasks you need to accomplish, how much time you have, and whose help you may need to accomplish your tasks. This is a normal routine for us all. So let's host meetings in the same manner. Have a point and communicate it.

"An agenda serves
as the roadmap that guides
discussion and ensures
that the meeting
remains focused."

4

HAVE AN AGENDA

DO YOU KNOW THE biggest reason people loathe meetings? They don't know what to expect when they go into them. They're blindsided.

Most meetings are completely unpredictable in terms of what will be discussed, how they will be conducted, or when they will end. When was the last time you were handed a meeting agenda prior to a meeting? It hardly ever happens. We're usually unsure of how long a meeting will last. We've all experienced a meeting that we thought would last for thirty minutes, but then two hours later, it still hasn't finished and there's no end in sight. It's the epitome of frustration. Indeed, meetings are the black holes of the business day. Nobody knows what's inside it, and once you're sucked in, it feels as if you can't get out!

Let me offer a personal example you can probably relate to. I once worked in an organization led by a disorganized extrovert who called meetings each week to help him brainstorm new ideas for the organization. It would always take a while for us to begin, because no one knew who was supposed to be in the meeting and what topic we were supposed to discuss. People would just trickle in when they were available, and they would chat about unrelated topics (i.e., sports, the weather) for a while. Then we would begin talking about our frustrations within the organization, with one or two individuals dominating that part of the conversation. Sometimes the entire meeting would become a complaint session. Other times, we'd get into a new initiative that seemed meaningful for the organization, but the leader would not want to discuss the details, so he would say that we should work on it outside of the meeting. So people were assigned to an initiative with no timetable or allocated resources. This created massive confusion about who was supposed to be working on each initiative, as the list would just grow with each meeting. Turnover at this company was high, and I personally blamed it on agenda-less meetings. They were the root cause of dysfunction and dissatisfaction.

How could these problems have been avoided or even solved? A meeting agenda would certainly have been a good start. Why does every meeting need an agenda?

People Like to Know What to Expect

We are undeniably a planning society, a people who find comfort and assurance in the act of meticulous preparation. From the moment we enter the world, we begin crafting blueprints for our lives. We plan our education, careers, and financial futures with precision, seeking to secure stability and success. We meticulously map out our personal journeys, from the grandeur of weddings and starting families to the tranquility of retirement. Our society thrives on calendars, schedules, and to-do lists, all designed to provide structure and direction to our daily lives. We are adept at anticipating challenges and have contingency plans for unforeseen hurdles. In the face of uncertainty, we seek solace in our well-thought-out plans, knowing they are the compass that guides us through the labyrinth of life's myriad choices and opportunities. Our penchant for planning reflects our innate desire to shape our destiny and navigate the unpredictable, reaffirming that planning is an integral part of our collective identity. Some of the things we plan:

- Estate
- Career
- Family size
- Retirement
- Vacation
- Savings

Let me offer a specific example that most people might relate to. If you think about a church service, for example, you generally know what's going to happen before you walk in and sit down. There's music, some announcements, and then the pastor or priest will offer a sermon or message. The length of the service is generally established, and there aren't often many surprises. Now imagine if the opposite were true. Imagine walking into a church having no idea the order of the service, how long it might last, or even what was going to happen. I'd venture to say that you'd never go to that church again if you couldn't predict what was going to happen inside the building. This is true of almost everything. When you sit down in a restaurant, the host hands you a menu. When you go into a theater to see a musical, you're handed a program. When you drive your car, your phone's GPS tells you specifically how long it will take to arrive at your destination. Imagine if it didn't.

You are probably agreeing with everything you just read. Am I correct? Yet most leaders don't take the time to adequately prepare for their own meetings. They are program-less and without purpose or chronology. They are agenda-less. If a meeting were a GPS device, it would be a blank screen without a voice!

Why don't leaders take the time to create a detailed agenda or fail to prioritize its distribution? This could be due to time constraints, no understanding of an agenda's importance, or simply a lack of organizational skills. Meetings may be more informal or spontaneous in some cases, with topics and discussions emerging on the spot. In such situations, it may not seem to be practical to create and distribute an agenda. In fact, in certain work cultures or environments, there may actually be a resistance to formalities, including the use of agendas. Some leaders perceive agendas as bureaucratic or unnecessary, preferring a more spontaneous approach to meetings. Nothing could be less true.

Sometimes a leader will call a meeting and just hope everything will come together. I call this the "emergency meeting," and it's common in today's business environment. This is the "let's see what happens" approach. The leader is hopeful that if everyone sits down together in the same room at the same time, somehow everything will fall together and it will be organized and productive. In a creative environment, this approach may work. In other words, if the only objective in a meeting is to be creative, a casual approach might work well, because it allows people the freedom to be creative and out-of-the-box. But this is not often the reason to have a meeting. Meetings are usually called to communicate something specific and solve problems. And it's not very often that problem solving simply emerges without some organized direction.

Some leaders also exhibit too much overconfidence going into a meeting, or they have an assumption of shared understanding. They assume that all participants have a clear understanding of the meeting's purpose and the topics to be discussed. They may believe that an agenda is unnecessary because everyone is already on the same page. However, this assumption often leads to confusion, miscommunication, and inefficiency. The problem is that some participants may run with their own agendas, leaving others behind or causing tension. It's not often that everyone is on the same page going into a meeting. The opposite is almost always the case, and leaders should assume a meeting may have multiple agendas running through people's heads if they don't provide one.

I also believe that in some cases, some leaders may actually resist being held accountable for sticking to a predetermined agenda. They prefer the flexibility to deviate from the planned topics or to address issues as they arise during the meeting only to protect themselves from having to lead and be productive. They hide behind the lack of communication. While flexibility can be important, it's more important for the leader to act as if the solution depends on the success of the meeting. A leader should be held accountable for a meeting's success, and the lack of an agenda will result in no accountability because there's no plan. Leaders are held accountable in so many other ways in a business environment. Why not also with how they manage their meetings?

This gets to the core reason behind the purpose of an agenda: The plan. In the last chapter, I shared the importance of having a "point" going into a meeting. But a point without a plan won't get you very far.

There are many good books about planning and the planning process. Of course, this is not a project management or planning book, so I won't take a deep dive into its importance. But there's an old adage that says, "Life is what happens to us while we are making other plans." The same holds true for meetings. If there's no plan and no agenda, they will just happen. And if they just happen, most everything else surrounding the meeting will just happen as well.

The bottom line is that an agenda is paramount for the success of any meeting. It serves as the roadmap that not only guides the discussion but also ensures that the gathering remains focused and productive. An agenda clarifies the meeting's purpose, sets clear objectives, and allocates time for each topic, preventing discussions from veering off track. It allows participants to come prepared, giving them a chance to gather relevant information and ideas in advance, ultimately leading to more informed and meaningful contributions. Moreover, an agenda promotes accountability, as it assigns responsibilities and deadlines for various agenda items. In essence, a well-structured agenda is a powerful planning tool that maximizes efficiency, fosters engagement, and helps achieve the desired outcomes, making it an indispensable component of any successful meeting.

Why is planning important?

- Planning helps us identify our goals clearly. It makes us decide concretely what we need to do to reach our core objectives. Likewise, an agenda.
- Planning helps assure us that we all understand our goal and what we need to do to reach it by involving everyone in the planning process. Likewise, an agenda.
- Planning makes us all work in a goal-oriented manner rather than in a loose or ad-hoc way in which we just respond to issues and crises with no clear plan or goal. Likewise, an agenda.
- Planning helps us see in advance the assignments that can help us achieve our goal and the obstacles that can prevent us from achieving our goal and work out what to do about them. Likewise, an agenda.
- Planning helps us to be accountable for what we do. Likewise an agenda.
- Finally, planning lays the basis for us to assess and evaluate our achievements effectively. Likewise, an agenda.

An agenda is simply a plan. Effective leaders always have a plan. That goes without saying, and few leaders would argue with me. Yet many leaders don't have plans for their own meetings. While many other items and actions are planned out, sometimes even meticulously, they fail to plan their meetings.

Tactical Ways to Create Effective Meeting Agendas

Creating an effective meeting agenda doesn't have to be a complex or arduous task. Simplicity often paves the way for efficiency and effectiveness. Contrary to the misconception that crafting a meeting agenda is a complex endeavor, creating a clear and concise meeting agenda can be a seamless task that not only saves time but also ensures that your meetings are purposeful and productive. In fact, you can streamline the process by focusing on three key tactical actions that will help you craft agendas that keep meetings on track and participants engaged.

A well-structured meeting agenda should be concise, easy to follow, and distributed to all participants in advance. To craft an impactful meeting agenda, start by clearly defining the purpose. What are the objectives you aim to achieve? Once you have a clear goal in mind, identify the key topics that need to be discussed to reach those objectives. Be specific, and prioritize the most important items. Next, allocate time slots for each agenda item to ensure the meeting stays on track. And as the meeting leader, don't hesitate to enforce those time limits. It not only keeps the meeting on schedule but also demonstrates your commitment to efficiency and respect for participants' time. By doing so, you will foster an environment in which discussions remain productive and on point. We'll get into this more later in this book.

You might also want to assign responsibilities to individuals for leading discussions or presenting information, fostering a sense of ownership and participation. When appropriate, include any necessary background materials or documents that participants should review before the meeting.

Finally, try to distribute an agenda several days before a meeting. It signals to participants that you respect their time and commitments. It allows them to review the agenda, prepare their contributions, and plan their schedules accordingly. Surprise meetings or those with last-minute agendas should be the exception rather than the rule. While spontaneity has its place, it should be reserved for rare situations or short, urgent meetings. A well-delivered agenda in advance helps participants come to the meeting prepared and informed.

Providing individuals with sufficient time to prepare for their designated agenda segments is crucial. Even if you allocate an hour or two for preparation, it can significantly enhance the quality of their contributions. Most people prefer not to provide extemporaneous feedback in meetings, so allowing them preparation time is essential.

Does this sound too complicated or time-consuming? It's certainly not as complicated and time-consuming as most meetings. You'll actually save time when you craft and distribute agendas in advance. Creating effective meeting agendas can elevate the quality of your meetings and ensure that they remain productive, purposeful, and well-received by participants. They will give the participants the confidence they need going into the meetings. An agenda will also put everyone at rest that a meeting won't last too long.

"Effective meeting dynamics
enables you to navigate
conflicts constructively."

5

MASTER MEETING DYNAMICS

PURPOSE AND AGENDAS WILL set the stage for more productive meetings. But they are only part of the equation. The management of meeting dynamics constitutes another critical facet that profoundly influences the overall success and productivity of your gatherings. Understanding and skillfully navigating the dynamics of a meeting is essential because every person who participates brings a unique background, perspective, and personality. Treating all participants the same, without recognizing and adapting to their individual differences, can hinder your ability to achieve the desired results.

Mastering meeting dynamics is essential because even with a well-crafted agenda, a meeting can fall flat if participants are not actively engaged. Mastering meeting dynamics involves creating an environment in which everyone feels comfortable sharing thoughts, ideas, and concerns. It means encouraging open dialogue, actively listening to participants, and promoting inclusivity. It also often means navigating conflict. Meetings often involve discussions with differing opinions and conflicting viewpoints. Effective meeting dynamics enable you to navigate these conflicts constructively. You'll need skills in conflict resolution, diplomacy, and effective guidance toward mutually beneficial outcomes.

You'll need to:

- Manage energy levels, because understanding meeting dynamics allows you to gauge the energy levels of participants and make adjustments as needed. For instance, you can incorporate interactive activities, breaks, or changes in format to keep participants refreshed.
- Build consensus when disagreements arise. You must be adept at facilitating discussions, summarizing key points, and guiding the group toward consensus or a resolution. Effective decision-making processes are an essential part of productive meetings.
- Handle unexpected disruptions when they arise, whether technical issues or disorderly behavior. Mastering meeting dynamics means being prepared to handle such disruptions swiftly and professionally, ensuring minimal interruptions to the agenda and flow of the meeting.

- Maintain focus and keep meetings on track and focused on the agenda, which requires skillful management of the dynamics. You'll need to redirect off-topic discussions, encourage participants to stick to time limits, and ensure that the objectives are met.
- Master meeting dynamics in virtual meetings, which are increasingly common in today's business landscape. This involves understanding the unique challenges and opportunities of online meetings, such as managing technology and addressing distractions.

Thousands of books and resources are available today on the topic of managing diverse personalities, but very few (if any) specifically address managing diverse personalities during meetings. So in this chapter, I'll look at ten distinct personalities that have the potential to significantly influence meeting dynamics. My aim is to provide insights and strategies that will empower you to harness their strengths and effectively mitigate their weaknesses. From the verbose Loud Guy to the introverted Quiet Guy, each personality type brings a unique set of characteristics, motivations, strengths, and challenges to the meeting table. By gaining a deeper understanding of these personalities and their roles, you can enhance your ability to create a more productive and engaging meeting experience.

There is sometimes danger in relying too much on any personality profile assessments because of the illusion of certainty they can create. Personality assessments often assign individuals to fixed categories or labels, and if misused, they can reinforce stereotypes and biases. So while I'm careful not to oversimplify, I think that you'll recognize each of these people, and truth be told, you are probably one of them. Also (and this is important), none of these meeting personality profiles should be viewed in a negative light. By recognizing the value of each of their contributions and by leveraging their unique talents, you can create a collaborative and inclusive meeting environment.

Leveraging the Verbal Processor

The Verbal Processor, a distinct meeting personality, possesses a natural inclination to externalize thoughts and ideas. These individuals feel an internal pressure to express every thought, often resulting in a high level of verbal participation during meetings. They talk, and talk, and talk, often dominating the meeting. This can be frustrating to the meeting leader and to the group as a whole. However, their tendency to externalize their thoughts can be a valuable asset in driving collaboration and generating diverse perspectives.

By actively soliciting their input, asking open-ended questions, and encouraging them to provide concise summaries of their ideas, you can help Verbal Processors contribute in a way that adds value to the meeting discussion without dominating the conversation. I try to gently redirect their focus or provide time limits for individual responses, thereby ensuring that their contributions remain valuable while maintaining a balanced meeting atmosphere. And by encouraging other participants to actively engage with the Verbal Processors' thoughts, providing constructive feedback, and encouraging diverse perspectives, you can harness the power of their communication style to foster robust discussions.

Sometimes it can be challenging to shut down or even slow down Verbal Processors, but it's truly imperative to do so. Otherwise, a meeting can go completely in a different direction. It may warrant a conversation pre- or post-meeting to ensure that these individuals allow for others to contribute to the meeting as well. At the same time, remember that they can be instrumental during a meeting to get everyone else talking as well.

Tapping into the Note-Taker

The Note-Taker, an often overlooked meeting personality, possesses a remarkable talent for capturing the essence of a meeting through diligent note-taking. These participants are often quiet and meticulous, but they can also be confusing because they may not outwardly contribute much, yet they still seem quite engaged. It's easy to ignore them and dismiss the notion that they might be a real asset during a meeting. While the presence of Note-Takers may be perceived as passive, it is essential to recognize and elevate their contributions.

When you strive to use the Note-Takers' comprehensive notes as valuable resources to foster accountability within the team, you will gain valuable insights into transforming their presence from passive to active contributors. Note-Taking is an essential skill that allows one to distill complex discussions, ideas, and action items into concise and organized notes. From the ability to capture key points, document decisions, and create a record of the meeting, Note-Takers can serve as valuable resources for the entire team.

When you encourage Note-Takers to share their insights, to ask clarifying questions, or to provide summaries of key points, you can tap into their understanding of the meeting's objectives and promote their active engagement. You might also consider asking them to share their notes promptly after the meeting so team members can refer to important information. This may clarify any misunderstandings and ensure alignment on action items.

Unleashing the Power of the Quiet Guy

Quiet Guys may seem disengaged and uninterested, but beneath their calm exterior lies a treasure trove of insights and reflections. Introverts often thrive in quieter, more contemplative settings where they can process information internally before sharing their thoughts, so they naturally tend to shut down in small group environments. The soft-spoken nature of Quiet Guys can sometimes cause their contributions to be overlooked or unheard in more vocal discussions.

However, the introverted nature of Quiet Guys should not be mistaken for disengagement but rather recognized as a source of valuable insights and reflections. By creating an inclusive environment, amplifying their voice, intentionally appreciating their thoughtful contributions, and encouraging pre-meeting preparation, you can unleash the full power of Quiet Guys. By embracing and valuing introversion, you can foster a culture of deep collaboration that benefits the entire team and drives innovation.

It's a bit tricky sometimes to make Quiet Guys comfortable enough to contribute. But as the meeting leader, if you try to actively seek their input, invite them to speak early in discussions, and even provide platforms for written or anonymous contributions, you'll make great strides. They typically don't like to be in the spotlight, but given some gentle coaxing and encouragement, and by understanding their need for reflection and recognizing the value they bring, you can create a space that honors their unique strengths. Structure is also important to introverts, so don't make the mistake of making your meetings too open-ended.

Navigating the One-Upper's Competitive Spirit

In many meetings there may be individuals who consistently present themselves as having better ideas than everyone else. I refer to them as the One-Uppers; they are driven by a competitive spirit that can hinder collaboration and stifle open dialogue. They can be particularly difficult to manage during a meeting because their contributions can be off-putting to the other participants. Nobody likes to hear that their ideas are bad, particularly in front of other people.

To effectively deal with One-Uppers, it is crucial to understand their motivations and underlying reasons for constantly seeking to outdo others. By recognizing that their competitive nature may stem from a desire to gain recognition, assert their expertise, or demonstrate value, you can approach their contributions with empathy and devise strategies to redirect their energies toward more collaborative endeavors. It's important to acknowledge their input with optimism, but also offer some balance and foster continued collaboration with the team.

In fact, one of the key strategies for dealing with One-Uppers is to shift the focus from competition to collaboration. By emphasizing the value of diverse perspectives and highlighting the collective goal of the meeting, you can channel the competitive spirit of One-Uppers toward collaborative problem-solving, ultimately leading to more innovative and effective outcomes. Another essential technique for navigating the behavior of One-Uppers is to practice active listening and empathetic communication. By harnessing their drive and channeling it toward problem-solving, you can unlock their potential as a catalyst for innovation and create a more harmonious meeting environment.

Harnessing the Affirmer's Influence

Affirmers, with their penchant for praise and positive feedback, have the power to uplift and motivate others. They are super optimistic and always happy, and they often nod in agreement during meetings. As a meeting leader, Affirmers are positive influences and are often fun to have in meetings. Learn to leverage Affirmers to improve your meetings, but also watch out for their tendency toward unrealistic or over-optimism.

Affirmers, with their natural inclination for praise and positive feedback, possess the remarkable ability to uplift and motivate others. By embracing their affirmations and using them strategically, you will inspire greater confidence, drive, and cohesion, ultimately leading to improved team performance and a more positive work environment. By acknowledging the importance of positive feedback and recognizing the unique strengths that Affirmers bring, you can harness their abilities to create an atmosphere of encouragement and recognition.

While affirmations are powerful, it's also important to keep their optimism in check. You don't want Affirmers to convince the group that there aren't problems to solve. Use them strategically to maximize their impact, but at the same time, don't allow them to influence others toward laziness or apathy. Meetings are places where problems need to be exposed and solved. And while optimism is a good thing, it has a dark side too. Not only can it lead to poor outcomes, but it can also cause us to underestimate risks or to take less action. I've noticed that people with overly good moods can be particularly annoying for those who are predisposed with overly bad moods! So try to find a balance during the meetings.

Humoring the Jokester

Jokesters, renowned for their ability to inject humor and lightheartedness into meetings, play a valuable role in providing a much-needed respite from the intensity of business discussions. Humor holds a remarkable power to transform the atmosphere and dynamics of meetings. By recognizing the ability of Jokesters to lighten the mood and improve engagement, you can create an environment where individuals feel more comfortable expressing their ideas, collaborating with others, and fostering team cohesion. But if not well-managed, humor can also spell disaster for your meeting.

While the Jokesters' humor can be a valuable asset, it is crucial to strike a balance that aligns with the meeting objectives. It's important to respect boundaries and sensitivities within the team. By promoting an inclusive and respectful approach to humor, you can ensure that the contributions of Jokesters will uplift and unite the team but also foster an atmosphere of inclusivity, trust, and mutual respect.

Also, by setting clear meeting agendas, understanding the desired outcomes, and employing humor strategically, you can ensure that the Jokesters' contributions enhance the meeting's effectiveness and maintain a productive atmosphere. By striking the right balance, you can leverage the Jokesters' unique talents to create a positive and productive meeting environment that drives success. So laugh along, but try not to laugh for too long!

Engaging the Story-Teller

There's a Story-Teller in every meeting, someone who decides to tell the group every single detail about a particular person, place, or event. While the stories can be interesting, they can also be irrelevant. Story-Tellers possess a unique talent for weaving captivating narratives that have the power to inspire and educate, but they can also distract. By establishing guidelines for storytelling relevance and brevity, you can strike a balance between captivating narratives and efficient meeting outcomes, maximizing the value of the Story-Tellers' contributions.

Storytelling has been a fundamental means of communication throughout human history. By recognizing the Story-Tellers' ability to captivate attention and evoke emotions, you can harness their skills to create memorable and impactful meeting experiences. But to engage Story-Tellers effectively, it is crucial to leverage their storytelling abilities to enhance meeting engagement. While storytelling can be powerful, it is important to establish guidelines for relevance and brevity to ensure that meetings stay focused and efficient.

By setting expectations for storytelling relevance, time limits, and alignment with meeting agenda, you can encourage Story-Tellers to share their stories in a way that enhances the overall meeting experience without derailing discussions or prolonging the meeting.

Overcoming the Downer's Negativity

Downers, known for skepticism and a negative outlook, can dampen the enthusiasm and productivity of any meeting. These individuals have a way of looking at things from a "the glass-is-half-empty" perspective, finding fault with almost anything or anyone. The negativity can be too much at times, which can make it hard for a meeting leader to manage. But by reframing their mindset and leveraging their critical thinking skills, you can harness the ability of Downers to identify potential pitfalls while maintaining an optimistic and solutions-oriented approach.

Constructive criticism plays a vital role in improving outcomes and avoiding potential pitfalls.

By recognizing the Downers' critical thinking skills and their ability to identify potential challenges, you can leverage their insights to enhance the team's decision-making and problem-solving abilities. To transform the Downers' pessimism into a constructive mindset, it is crucial to reframe their perspective. By encouraging them to focus on providing solutions along with identifying challenges, you can channel their critical thinking skills in a positive direction.

Through effective techniques and a supportive environment, you can turn skepticism into a valuable asset for the team. By encouraging this person to examine issues from different angles, consider alternative perspectives, and engage in collaborative problem-solving, you can tap into their ability to identify potential pitfalls and risks. While addressing potential pitfalls and challenges, it is important to maintain an optimistic and solutions-oriented approach.

Empowering the Busy Guy

The Busy Guy, known for always being preoccupied and distracted, can hinder productivity and impede meeting efficiency. Busy Guys arrive late to meetings, seem disheveled, are often multi-tasking, and often look at both phone and cell phone. The perpetual busyness can create challenges in engaging them fully during meetings.

To effectively engage Busy Guys, it is essential to foster a culture of time management within the team and organization. By creating a culture that values punctuality and respects everyone's time, you can encourage Busy Guys to prioritize and fully engage in meetings. Clear expectations play a crucial role in engaging Busy Guys and maximizing their participation. By providing them with a clear understanding of their role, their input, and the specific value they bring to the meeting, you can enhance their engagement and ensure their contributions align with the meeting's purpose. Also, by setting ground rules for meeting etiquette, encouraging active listening, and keeping discussions on track, you can create an environment that maximizes productivity and minimizes time wastage.

Engaging Busy Guys requires strategies to promote their active participation during meetings. By actively involving them and acknowledging the value of their insights, you can motivate them to be fully present and contribute meaningfully to meeting discussions.

Mastering Meeting Harmony

Again, I caution against over-simplification. Each of these personalities is actually not as well-defined or recognizable as I just made it appear. There is overlap, and each of us brings multiple personalities to the meetings we attend and those we manage. But by embracing the unique strengths while mitigating the challenges of each individual, you can create an environment that fosters collaboration, creativity, and high performance in your meetings. By simply embracing the unique strengths and perspectives of each person, you can create a more inclusive and innovative meeting environment. This means actively seeking diverse voices, encouraging participation from all team members, and fostering a culture that values and celebrates differences. When you leverage the collective intelligence and diverse perspectives of your team, you can unlock new insights, drive creativity, and make more informed decisions.

"One of the biggest mistakes
that meeting leaders make is
to assume that people want
to be there in the first place."

6

CULTIVATING PARTICIPATION

ACTIVE PARTICIPATION IN A meeting is not an automatic occurrence; it requires intention and effort from all attendees. It involves more than just physically being in the room; it also demands engaging, listening, and contributing constructively to the discussions. Effective meetings are a collaborative effort where individuals come prepared, ask questions, share insights, and work collectively toward the meeting's objectives. Without this proactive involvement, meetings can devolve into unproductive gatherings, leaving important matters unresolved and diminishing their overall value to the organization.

One of the biggest mistakes that meeting leaders make is to assume that people want to be there in the first place, and if not, they certainly don't want to participate in the meeting. Sitting in a meeting is one thing, while actually speaking is quite another. Even under the best case scenarios, most people shy away from active engagement during meetings.

Several factors discourage people from actively participating and sharing during meetings.

One of the primary reasons individuals tend to shy away from active participation in meetings is due to a lack of psychological safety, or in other words, the fear of judgment or criticism. Ask yourself this question: How many times have you silently decided not to say something in a meeting, simply because you were afraid of how people might respond? I think we'd all admit to doing this on at least one occasion, and probably many. This apprehension can paralyze even the most articulate of team members. People are often concerned that when they share their opinions, their ideas may be met with disdain, ridicule, or dismissal. The dread of having their contributions labeled as insignificant or incorrect can stifle creativity and innovation during a meeting. It's a natural human instinct to want to avoid discomfort or embarrassment, and this fear can cause valuable perspectives to remain unspoken. This fear of embarrassment can breed a culture of silence, where vital issues remain unaddressed and opportunities for real dialogue are missed.

But there are other reasons as well. In time-pressed meetings, participants might prioritize efficiency over discussion, opting to keep their remarks brief or abstain from speaking altogether. Time is a precious commodity in the workplace, and everyone has personal issues to tend to. During a meeting, people are very much aware of how much time is passing, how much work is waiting for them after the meeting, and also what's in store for them after work.

Our instant access to communication during meetings exacerbates this problem, as our phones are blowing up with text messages and notifications. Sometimes people will silently hope that if they stay quiet, the meeting will end sooner. And indeed it will end sooner, but the problem is that the meeting becomes unproductive as issues remain undiscussed and unresolved. I find that meeting leaders underestimate this problem and often ignore it entirely. I'll share a simple solution later in this chapter, which includes asking participants to leave their phones outside the meeting room.

A third reason people tend not to participate in meetings is that when individuals perceive that decisions have already been made without their input, it often serves as a demotivating factor, leading to their reluctance to actively engage. This sense of predetermined outcomes can manifest in various ways, causing individuals to question the relevance of their contributions. They might think, "Why should I voice my opinion when it won't make any difference?" This sentiment can lead to a feeling of powerlessness, where their input seems inconsequential in shaping the final decisions. Consequently, these individuals may choose to disengage or become passive observers, believing that their involvement won't have any impact on the outcome. This situation not only stifles their potential contributions but can also diminish their sense of ownership and commitment to the meeting's goals.

Certainly, there are instances when a more open-ended and freeform brainstorming session becomes not just beneficial but essential. Creativity often thrives when there's room to freely shout out ideas, and too rigid an agenda can stifle innovation. During such occasions, inviting meeting participants to engage in a creative idea-sharing exercise where they can freely contribute their thoughts can prove both effective and enjoyable for all involved. In these moments, the atmosphere can become electric with the potential for breakthroughs! Yet, even in these creative bursts, maintaining control over the meeting's direction is important. It's essential not to let the flow of ideas turn into a chaotic free-for-all that derails the meeting's purpose. To strike the right balance, a skilled meeting leader should provide a loose framework for the brainstorming session. This framework might include setting clear objectives, defining the scope of the discussion, and gently guiding the conversation to ensure that the generated ideas remain relevant to the meeting's goals. While encouraging creativity, the leader should also keep an eye on the clock to ensure that the meeting stays on track.

So there are several stifling dynamics at work during a meeting, and unless the leader possesses an awareness of these dynamics, there's a significant risk that participation will remain limited and of subpar quality, leading to missed opportunities for collaboration and problem-solving.

How to Encourage Active Participation

First and foremost, fostering active participation should be regarded as an essential mandate during a meeting. Frankly, there shouldn't be a way out. Everyone in a meeting should have a minimum contribution. It's the leader's way of saying, "You're here because we want you here; you're important to us and we need your contribution." I strongly believe that a stated minimum contribution actually gives participants more confidence, not less, because their inputs are clearly valued by the leader. And if some people can't or won't contribute, they probably shouldn't be in the meeting in the first place. Meetings are not places to receive information. That's what emails are for. Meetings are for dialogue. So a leader's goal should be to expect comments from everyone at the table.

If a team member refuses to participate in meetings, then that person might not be a good fit for the organization. Or you, as the leader, might be failing to set a vision that the individual understands. Take time to assess the root of the problem and take action. The bottom line is that all team members must participate in the meetings they attend.

For every meeting that I facilitate, I place a strong emphasis on the requirement for active involvement. I briefly talk about it at the beginning of every meeting. It is my practice to clearly articulate to all attendees that their contributions are not just encouraged, but expected. I believe this expectation sets a precedent for engagement and underscores the idea that every participant has a vital role to play in the meeting's success. By making this stance explicit, I aim to create an environment in which individuals feel accountable for contributing their insights and perspectives, thereby ensuring that the meeting is a collaborative and productive forum. I ask that each participant offers at least two comments during every meeting.

Requiring active participation doesn't end there. You also must actively protect everyone's psychological safety. This is crucial for creating an environment in which individuals feel comfortable sharing their thoughts and concerns without fear of negative consequences. Otherwise, you'll end up with an even worse situation. Requiring everyone to talk, and then allowing for unreasonable criticism, will backfire and end in an unproductive meeting.

Make People Feel Safe and Confident During Meetings

It's important to establish ground rules that emphasize respect, active listening, and open-mindedness. One of your primary goals as a meeting leader is to make all attendees feel that they can participate without negative ramifications. It's not hard, yet it is often ignored. Here's how I recommend you get there with ease.

First, clearly communicate that all contributions are valued and will be treated with respect. If this is left unsaid, the anxiety levels will rise in the room. But if you set the stage for respectful communication, you'll find people to be more comfortable when they contribute. As the leader, you can also demonstrate the desired behavior by actively listening to participants, acknowledging their input, and refraining from interrupting or belittling anyone's ideas. You will also accomplish this by recognizing and appreciating the input of participants, even if their ideas are not immediately adopted. This acknowledgment reinforces the value of their contributions.

Second, it's essential to recognize that drawing good feedback out of individuals may require a deliberate and thoughtful approach. Encouraging high-quality participation often involves more than merely requiring people to spontaneously share their thoughts.

Instead, a meeting leader may need to employ various strategies to create an environment where feedback feels not only welcome but also actively sought after. One effective technique is to ask open-ended questions that invite participants to express their viewpoints and experiences. These questions should encourage reflection and discussion rather than simple yes or no responses. Additionally, active listening plays a crucial role; leaders should attentively listen to what is being said, ask follow-up questions, and paraphrase to ensure they understand participants' perspectives accurately.

Recognizing nonverbal cues is also important. Many people do not feel confident in verbalizing their thoughts, but their body language, facial expressions, or tone of voice may provide valuable insights. A perceptive meeting leader can pick up on these cues and gently encourage further discussion. Great leaders are attuned to non-verbal cues. Work at it and it will pay off.

In essence, being intentional in drawing feedback from participants involves creating a safe, inclusive, and engaging space where contributions are valued and where individuals are encouraged to share their thoughts through various means, ensuring that their voices are heard and respected. This is not to say participants should hold back from offering constructive conflict. It's a good thing to encourage healthy debate and differing viewpoints, but then also ensure that it remains respectful and focused on the issues rather than becoming personal.

Finally (and I've already shared this in the previous chapter), it's imperative to understand that people's willingness to contribute is significantly influenced by their awareness of when the meeting will end. This simple concept underscores the importance of efficient time management. When a meeting stretches endlessly without a clear endpoint, participants often find their enthusiasm waning, leading them to become progressively less engaged and forthcoming with their input. As such, every meeting agenda should clearly offer participants when the session will both begin and end. In essence, the human psyche thrives on structure and predictability. Setting a timeframe not only respects participants' schedules and commitments but also provides a sense of direction and purpose. It sets expectations for how long the discussion will last and assures participants that their time is being respected. This, in turn, encourages individuals to be more proactive in contributing their insights, knowing that their efforts will not be in vain during a never-ending meeting.

There are certainly many ways to manage time, but I've discovered a simple rule that works in almost every meeting: Communicate specifically when it will end, and then also communicate how much time will be spent discussing each separate issue. It's truly that simple. And don't violate your commitment. I believe if every leader did this at the outset of every meeting, it would revolutionize results. Your team will love you for it and will help turn your meetings around.

Remember, you can always have another meeting if there are unresolved issues. The worst meetings are those in which people simply refuse to participate. The silence is deafening. But if you cultivate participation, you'll find the end result will be positive in that you'll be closer to solving problems and achieving your goals.

"Rather than viewing conflict as a detriment, savvy leaders recognize it as an opportunity for growth."

7

FACILITATING CONFLICT RESOLUTION

CONFLICT IS AN INHERENT part of human interaction, and it often finds its way into meetings, where diverse perspectives, competing interests, and passionate discussions can lead to disagreements. Sometimes it does not matter how well you're prepared for a meeting; conflict can emerge, sometimes in a sudden and messy way. It can be hard to predict, and each participant will react in a different way.

When an ugly conflict arises at a meeting, the atmosphere in the room can become tense and uncomfortable. Participants with differing viewpoints can become increasingly vocal and passionate about their positions. Voices may start to rise in volume, and body language can become more defensive. The conflict may escalate into a verbal confrontation, with participants directly challenging each other's ideas, decisions, or statements. Accusations, blame, and pointed criticisms may be exchanged. Participants may interrupt one another, making it difficult for anyone to speak. This further contributes to the chaotic and confrontational atmosphere. They may use gestures to emphasize their points or to express frustration. These gestures can range from finger-pointing to hand-waving and even pounding the table for emphasis, with their defensive body language becoming more pronounced. Some participants may cross their arms, lean away from each other, or physically distance themselves from those they're in conflict with.

How I Learned the Hard Way

We've all experienced conflicts during meetings. I know I certainly have. Prior to launching my company, Six Figure Dinners, I co-founded and operated a food service business. Starting with a single food truck, we eventually operated eleven Menchie's Frozen Yogurt locations, alongside a Menchie's food truck, situated within the thriving Houston, Texas, metropolitan region. This venture entailed a meticulously executed 36-month real estate search and build-out strategy, resulting in the successful development of these establishments. Our primary objective was to position Menchie's as the preferred community gathering place for families and children, which we accomplished through strategic marketing efforts and active engagement with the local community. To maintain exceptional customer service, I personally oversaw the recruitment, hiring, and comprehensive training of hundreds of team members and store leaders.

The operation and expansion of the food-service business involved a multitude of meetings, ranging from informal discussions to substantial gatherings. I vividly recall one particular ad-hoc meeting, in which I aimed to provide a well-intentioned dose of constructive criticism to a dedicated store manager. In my assessment, my tone and delivery remained reasonably composed, but to my surprise, my feedback was met with a vehement eruption of anger from the manager. The ensuing argument unfolded with astonishing intensity, casting a shadow over the entire meeting room. In that moment, I found myself immobilized, grappling with uncertainty about how to respond or proceed. In the aftermath, we did manage to navigate our differences, and in the ensuing days and weeks, our working relationship gradually improved. However, it was undeniable that the incident had exacted a tangible toll on the dynamics and overall performance of the business, serving as a stark reminder of the delicate balance required in managing interpersonal relationships during meetings.

You've probably experienced your share of conflict during meetings. During conflict, meeting facilitators face a challenging dilemma. They may attempt to intervene to restore order and steer the discussion toward a more constructive path. However, this can be a delicate balancing act, as they try to remain impartial while addressing the conflict. The conflict may reach a point where it becomes a stalemate, with neither side willing to budge or compromise. This can result in an impasse that stalls progress on the meeting's agenda. The hostile emotions, such as anger, frustration, and even tears, may surface and make it even more difficult to manage. Needless to say, the original purpose and agenda of the meeting becomes overshadowed by the conflict, leading to a sense of wasted time and frustration.

In this chapter, we'll explore the art of facilitating effective conflict resolution during meetings, enabling teams to harness the positive potential of conflicts while maintaining a productive and harmonious environment. I'll share how you can avoid unhealthy conflict and also manage it when it becomes a detriment to the meeting's objectives. Notice that I said "unhealthy" conflict. Not all conflict during a meeting is a bad thing. Rather than viewing it as a detriment, savvy leaders recognize it as an opportunity for growth, innovation, and improved decision-making.

Conflict during Meetings Can Be a Good Thing

Conflict during a meeting can be a good thing for several reasons. First, it brings to light diverse perspectives and ideas, which can lead to more creative thinking and innovative solutions. When individuals with different viewpoints engage in constructive conflict, they are forced to critically evaluate their positions and consider alternative options, ultimately contributing to better decision-making. So even when new or contrarian views and opinions are offered in a less-than-constructive manner, it doesn't necessarily mean they're bad ideas.

Second, conflict stimulates engagement and active participation among meeting participants. This is not always a bad thing. People become more invested in the discussion when they need to defend their viewpoints or advocate for their ideas. This heightened engagement can lead to a more productive and focused meeting. You'd rather have a little conflict than silence with full cooperation. In fact, if you're not experiencing any conflict in your meetings, you might need to consider that your team isn't being honest with you or with each other.

Moreover, conflict provides an opportunity for individuals to develop and practice conflict resolution skills, including active listening, empathy, and negotiation. These skills are valuable not only in the context of the meeting but also in fostering better interpersonal relationships and teamwork. When managed effectively, conflict can strengthen relationships among meeting participants. Open and respectful communication during conflict resolution can foster trust, empathy, and mutual respect, which can lead to improved working relationships. This can spill over outside of meetings in a positive way.

Finally, always remember that conflict can hold individuals and teams accountable for their actions and decisions. When conflicts are addressed, responsibility is assigned, and actions are tracked, it can result in a higher level of accountability within the group, promoting transparency and accountability. But can happen only if you, the meeting facilitator, take charge. If not, the result will negatively impact your next team meeting. You'll start where you ended, with hurt feelings and hostile emotions.

Common Challenges in Conflict Resolution

Effective conflict resolution is a cornerstone of successful business operations, yet navigating these waters is often far from straightforward. In the pursuit of resolution, one must be prepared to confront and overcome several common challenges:

- **Resistance to resolution:** One of the foremost challenges in conflict resolution is encountering individuals who adamantly resist efforts to reach a compromise or solution. Such resistance can stem from deeply ingrained positions or unresolved personal grievances. In these instances, it is imperative to exercise patience and maintain persistent, open lines of communication. Encourage participants to express their concerns and viewpoints, emphasizing the importance of finding common ground.

- **Emotional intensity:** Conflicts frequently evoke strong emotions, which can easily derail rational discussions. As a facilitator or mediator, your role is pivotal in guiding participants toward managing their emotions constructively. Encourage them to acknowledge and validate their feelings while simultaneously directing their focus toward the core issues at hand. Techniques such as active listening and empathetic communication can help participants regain control over their emotional responses.

- **Cultural differences:** In today's diverse workplace environments, cultural disparities can significantly influence communication styles and responses to conflict. Recognizing and respecting these differences is essential. Approach conflict resolution with cultural sensitivity, and be prepared to address potential cross-cultural misunderstandings or clashes. Encourage open dialogue that allows team members to appreciate and learn from each other's diverse perspectives.

- **Power imbalances:** Power dynamics within a team can add layers of complexity to conflict resolution. It is crucial to ensure that all voices, regardless of rank or seniority, are not only heard but also genuinely valued. Foster an environment in which junior team members feel safe and empowered to voice their concerns without fear of repercussions. This can be achieved by implementing transparent and inclusive decision-making processes that give everyone an equal opportunity to contribute.

Effective conflict resolution during meetings requires a combination of interpersonal skills, communication strategies, and a structured approach. Here are key principles and techniques I've discovered that will help you better facilitate conflict resolution:

1. **Create a safe space:** The foundation of conflict resolution begins with establishing a secure meeting environment. Cultivate an atmosphere where participants feel comfortable expressing their opinions and concerns. Clearly communicate the value of respectful communication and active listening. Set ground rules that foster open dialogue and firmly discourage personal attacks or aggressive behavior.

2. **Understand the underlying issues:** Surface-level conflict resolution often falls short. To truly address conflicts effectively, you must delve into the root causes. Encourage all participants to articulate their perspectives and

motivations openly. Probe deeply to uncover underlying issues or concerns that may not be immediately apparent.

3. **Active listening:** The cornerstone of conflict resolution is active listening. Ensure that all participants have uninterrupted opportunities to speak, allowing them to feel genuinely heard. Reflect back what you've heard to confirm understanding and validate their viewpoints.

4. **Stay neutral and impartial:** As the facilitator or leader, maintaining a position of neutrality and impartiality is paramount. Avoid taking sides or displaying favoritism. Your role is to guide the process and ensure fairness.

5. **Reframe conflicts as opportunities:** Encourage participants to shift their perspective, viewing conflicts as opportunities for growth and improvement. Help them see disagreements as a chance to explore new ideas, gain insights, and collaboratively arrive at better solutions.

6. **Collaborative problem-solving:** Transition from a focus on "winning the argument" to collaborative problem-solving. Foster an environment in which participants work together to identify mutually beneficial solutions. Techniques such as brainstorming, consensus-building, and compromise are invaluable in this context.

7. **Use facilitation techniques:** Consider employing facilitation techniques such as role-playing, scenario analysis, or structured group discussions. These methods provide a framework for exploring alternatives and finding common ground.

9. **Document agreements:** Once resolutions are reached, document the agreements, action items, and responsibilities meticulously. This practice ensures clarity and accountability after the meeting. Share the documented outcomes with all relevant participants.

10. **Follow-up:** Effective conflict resolution doesn't conclude with the meeting. Schedule follow-up sessions or check-ins to evaluate progress in implementing agreed-upon solutions. Continuously monitor the situation to ensure that conflicts are genuinely resolved.

Effective conflict resolution during meetings is a valuable skill that can transform conflicts into opportunities for growth, collaboration, and improved decision-making. By creating a safe and respectful meeting environment, listening actively, and facilitating collaborative problem-solving, you can navigate conflicts successfully.

Remember that conflicts are natural in human interactions, and their presence doesn't signify failure. Instead, view them as catalysts for innovation and progress. As a leader or meeting facilitator, your ability to guide participants through conflict resolution processes will contribute to a more harmonious, productive, and successful team dynamic. Embrace conflict as a chance to elevate your team's performance and strengthen relationships, ultimately leading to better outcomes for your organization.

"Time limits provide a sense of urgency, encouraging participants to prioritize and align their contributions."

8

MANAGING TIME EFFECTIVELY

WHILE WE'D ALL LIKE to believe that we can juggle multiple tasks simultaneously and squeeze unlimited productivity out of our limited hours, reality does not always work out that way. Our brains aren't designed for this constant switching of attention. In fact, studies have shown that multitasking can lead to decreased productivity, increased stress, and even reduced cognitive abilities. I believe that the myth of multitasking is something we all eventually admit to. The more balls we drop, the more anxiety sets in. It's a vicious circle. It's as if we're trying to fit more into an already overflowing hourglass, only to watch the sand slip away faster!

Then packed tightly into our busy days are meetings—many of them, and often very long. While we sit in a meeting, we cannot help but think of all the other things we need to juggle after it is over. "I don't have time for another meeting!" is something we grumble to ourselves every day of the week. How many times have you said this in the last month? Meetings take up too much of our time and add stress to our already jam-packed schedules. As this battle for our time rages on, it's easy to feel overwhelmed, and we often find ourselves stretched thin, struggling to maintain a semblance of balance.

We've touched on this in previous chapters, but now I want to share how you can substantially improve your meetings with better time management. This is a strategy that will undoubtedly bolster your business. By ensuring meetings are concise, focused, and efficient, you can harness the collective expertise of your team without wasting valuable time. This not only increases productivity and accelerates decision-making but also fosters a culture of respect for your employees' time, enhancing their satisfaction and work-life balance. With improved time management in meetings, you can allocate more resources to strategic planning, ultimately positioning your business for greater success in a competitive landscape while minimizing unnecessary stress and costs.

Most meetings suffer from poor time management, resulting in a cascade of negative consequences. Often, discussions drift off-topic, leading to extended meeting durations that squander valuable employee time. This inefficiency not only erodes productivity but also frustrates participants, diminishing their engagement and morale. Moreover, the failure to stick to agendas and timeframes can hinder effective decision-making, delay critical projects, and, in some cases, contribute to missed opportunities. The cumulative impact of poorly managed meetings is absolutely detrimental, draining resources, increasing stress, and impeding a company's ability to adapt and compete effectively in today's fast-paced business environment. Addressing this issue is paramount to unlocking the full potential of a team and fostering a culture of efficiency and accountability.

I've discovered that it all comes down to the lack of a clear timeline. Very often, participants have no idea how a meeting will break out. The absence of a clear timeline is possibly the biggest complaint I hear from meeting participants. I'm sure you've sat in many meetings that seem to go on endlessly and without any time constraint whatsoever. When this happens, how do you feel about the meeting leader? I'm quite sure you lose trust and confidence in that person's leadership abilities. The impact of such meetings on participants is not to be underestimated.

Consider the following dynamics at play when a meeting lacks a clear timeline:

- **Disorientation and frustration:** When a meeting lacks time management, participants can quickly become disoriented and frustrated. As it extends beyond its expected duration, individuals may find it increasingly challenging to remain engaged and attentive. The sense of frustration stems not only from the wasted time but also from the uncertainty of when the meeting will conclude.

- **Perception of ineffectiveness:** Participants often equate the length of a meeting with its effectiveness. In other words, the longer it drags on without clear progress or direction, the more likely participants are to perceive it as ineffective. This perception can cast doubt on the leadership capabilities of the person in charge.

- **Loss of trust:** Trust is a cornerstone of effective leadership, and it can be fragile. When a meeting leader fails to manage time effectively, trust can erode. Participants may question whether the leader values their time and even if the meeting has a clear purpose.

- **Diminished engagement:** Extended meetings can result in disengaged participants who mentally check out or become preoccupied with other tasks. This lack of engagement not only hinders the meeting's objectives but also reflects poorly on the meeting leader's capacity to maintain a dynamic and participatory environment.

- **Impact on productivity:** Prolonged meetings disrupt participants' schedules and workloads, potentially affecting their overall productivity.

When time is wasted in unproductive meetings, it can have a cascading effect on the completion of tasks and projects.

You might think all of the above is so obvious that it doesn't even need to be stated. You'd think so, but it's still a huge issue, and all of us who attend meetings recognize it.

To combat these issues, it is essential for the meeting leader to establish a clear timeline and employ effective time management strategies. By setting a realistic agenda with allocated time slots for each agenda item, the leader can ensure that discussions remain focused and productive. Time limits provide a sense of urgency, encouraging participants to make their points succinctly and prioritize their contributions to align with the meeting's objectives.

Additionally, the meeting leader should facilitate adherence to the timeline by actively managing the discussion flow and intervening when necessary to keep the meeting on track. This may involve redirecting tangential conversations, summarizing key points, and encouraging participants to stay within the allotted time for each agenda item. It's not always easy because it will appear that you are cutting some people off. But in the end, it will result in a better meeting and everyone will thank you for it.

I've learned to be almost militant about meeting timelines. I lay it all out and I stick to what I've said. People appreciate it, and it forces everyone to stay more engaged and get to the point. When you first begin to do this, it might seem overly rigid or otherwise restricting. But the opposite is actually true.

This is also true of meetings, simply because they take up so much of our time. They suck a lot of minutes out of our days. Hence, one of your most important goals as a leader is to understand the critical role that time management plays in the success of your meetings. In this chapter, we will explore why poor time management is so destructive to our businesses and to our lives in general, and conversely how well-structured meetings can become one of the cornerstones of productivity, creativity, and a less stressful environment.

Leaders vastly underestimate the cost of each meeting they host. Previously in this book, I shared how unproductive meetings come at a considerable cost to a business. Imagine a one-hour meeting, attended by ten employees, veering off-topic, lacking direction, and overstaying its welcome. In this case, ten hours, not one single hour, of productive work time is sacrificed, not to mention the cost of what could have been achieved during that period. So every time you host a meeting, don't think about just the time spent overall but also that of each individual meeting participant. Let that sink in when your meeting goes long and is unproductive!

I believe most meetings could literally be cut in half and still achieve the desired results, which increase productivity and go straight to the bottom line. Less time spent in meetings means more profit, making the organization more successful and its people happier.

Respecting the time of meeting participants is not only courteous but also a strategic imperative. As I just shared, time is a limited resource. Every participant in every meeting you host is thinking about the time spent in that meeting. They are all literally thinking, "I wish I didn't have to be in this long meeting." And if you don't respect their time, you'll come out of your meeting less respected. All too often, we often have a selfish attitude toward time; we expect other people to adjust their schedules around us. We assume that the world revolves around our own schedules, and we demand that others adjust their lives to accommodate us while we guard our daily routines with unwavering vigilance. This paradoxical approach to time, particularly during meetings, is not only unfair but also detrimental to our businesses and organization.

But when participants perceive that a meeting is well-organized, focused, and respectful of their time, they are more likely to be engaged, contribute meaningfully, and remain committed to achieving the meeting's objectives. Respecting other people's time means recognizing that their schedules are just as significant as your own. Just because you're leading a meeting does not mean you own everyone's time. In fact, one of our primary goals should be to protect it. It's their time, not yours. Remember, the preacher who finishes his sermon last finds the pews empty the following Sunday!

I believe there are three "wins" for leaders who find ways to manage time effectively during meetings.

Achieving Outcomes

Effective time management is not just about being efficient; it's also about achieving desired outcomes efficiently. Well-managed meetings are more likely to stay on track, accomplish their goals, and generate actionable results. Conversely, poorly managed meetings can lead to confusion, duplication of efforts, and a lack of clarity on next steps. A meeting is a means to an end; don't make it the end. Some leaders like to meet just for the sake of meeting. They believe hosting meetings is an important part of their job. I could not disagree more. Your goal should be to have as few meetings as possible, and for each meeting to be tied directly to outcomes.

Ensuring Engagement

Time management isn't just about keeping the meeting on schedule; it's also about ensuring that participants are engaged throughout. When meetings are efficiently managed, participants are more likely to stay attentive and contribute actively because they see the value in investing their time. So your goal as a meeting leader should be to solicit engagement from the participants, not to do most of the talking. If you find yourself doing most of the talking, you could have saved time by sending an email or holding a short stand-up session rather than a full-fledged meeting.

While I share elsewhere in this book how to produce engagement during meetings, your goal should be to not only increase engagement overall, but also to protect everyone's time. You want to increase high-quality engagement and put a stop to low-quality, time-wasting engagement. Your goal should be to encourage people to talk about the right things in a way that will achieve better outcomes in less time.

Decision Fatigue

Time management also plays a critical role in mitigating what I call "decision fatigue." By allocating specific time slots for decision-making and problem-solving in a meeting, you help participants maintain their cognitive freshness. Lengthy, unstructured meetings that drag on can lead to decision fatigue, resulting in suboptimal choices and a lack of consensus. Meetings should result in solutions, not more problems. If you find that they create more problems than they solve, then you're probably a victim of decision fatigue.

In many meetings where time isn't managed effectively, a common scenario unfolds: a participant responds to a question with yet another question, triggering a chain reaction where others chime in with their own questions. In this spiraling cycle, the original question often gets sidelined, and the discussion veers off course. Sometimes the topic will be very different from the reason the meeting was called in the first place. This is frustrating for the meeting leader, but the problem arose because no time constraints were placed. The leader is the main source of the problem, not the participants.

Clearly, time in meetings needs to be managed better. What steps can leaders take?

- **Set clear objectives:** Begin by defining clear objectives for the meeting. What decisions need to be made, and what outcomes are you aiming for? Having a well-defined purpose will help keep discussions focused and prevent unnecessary deliberations. Clear meeting objectives save time. And it doesn't take much time to be clear about your meeting's purpose.

- **Create agendas that include time:** For the purposes of time management, I believe that agendas should include a beginning time, an end time, and also time limitations for discussion topics throughout the meeting. Develop a detailed agenda that outlines the topics to be discussed and allocates specific time slots for each item.

- **Limit meeting duration:** The average business meeting lasts thirty-one to sixty minutes, but studies show that the optimal length is actually fifteen to twenty minutes. Despite this, 73 percent of meetings last longer than thirty minutes. While it's not imperative that you keep all of them short, as some issues certainly do require more discussion, every meeting needs a stated end time. Set a strict time limit and stick to it. Make it known that it will end on time, which encourages participants to stay on track and avoid veering into unrelated discussions.

- **Assign time slots:** Allocate a specific time slot for each agenda item. For more critical decisions, allocate more time; for less critical ones, allocate less. This ensures that the most important topics receive the necessary attention. Again, when you create time slots, you need to stick to them. When you do, participants will understand and cooperate. They will work hard to be succinct and efficient.

- **Facilitate efficient discussions:** As the meeting organizer or facilitator, it's your responsibility to keep discussions on track. Politely intervene if they start to go off-topic or if participants become overly verbose. Encourage concise and relevant contributions.

- **Prioritize decisions:** Not all decisions are equally important. Prioritize the ones that must be made during the meeting, and consider deferring less critical ones to a later time or assigning them to a smaller subgroup for further exploration. Not every single item needs to be resolved in every single meeting. Don't waste your time on issues that are not part of the primary objective. Once you find resolution during a meeting, or otherwise address the issue at hand, simply end it.

- **Take breaks:** If the meeting is lengthy, schedule short breaks to allow participants to recharge. Decision fatigue is more likely to set in during extended sessions, so brief intermissions can help maintain focus and energy. Never meet for more than one hour without a break. Breaks will alleviate fatigue and stress.

- **Follow up promptly:** After the meeting, distribute minutes and action items promptly.

This allows participants to act on decisions and reduces the chance of revisiting the same issues in subsequent sessions. This will keep the next meeting shorter. Again, your goal as a leader should be to make meeting times efficient. By following up, you're creating a culture for short yet highly effective meetings.

- **Reflect and improve:** Periodically review the effectiveness of your meetings. Seek feedback from participants on how to make them more efficient and less draining. Use this input to continually improve your management skills.

Time will either be your most precious ally or your greatest enemy. Respect it, manage it, and own it, and especially during meetings. I like what Tony Morgan, author, pastor, and business strategist, once wrote about time: "You get to decide where your time goes. You can either spend it moving forward, or you can spend it putting out fires. You decide. And if you don't decide, others will decide for you." It's not hard to make your meetings more effective with better time management, which is why I'm surprised more leaders don't try. I encourage you to try, and I promise you'll be surprised at the results.

"

"Business owners often
find themselves perched
at the summit of their
organizations, which might
look prestigious, but it can
also be remarkably isolating."

"

9

SIX FIGURE DINNERS

MY HOPE IS THAT by reading this book, you've gained invaluable insights and practical strategies to master the art of conducting productive, engaging, and purpose-driven meetings. I've shared how to create purpose and an agenda, navigate the complex dynamics of group interactions, leverage technology wisely, and skillfully facilitate conflict resolution. With these newfound skills, you will not only elevate the quality of your meetings but also inspire your team to greater heights. As a result, you will emerge as a more confident and influential leader, capable of harnessing the full potential of your team, fostering collaboration, and driving positive change within your organization.

I also promised to share with you about my business, Six Figure Dinners, which is truly the foundation from which I mastered the art of conducting productive meetings. I love the feedback I hear from our members after our meetings.

"Six Figure Dinners has been honestly incredible. I finally feel like I'm not alone. Each person gets a chance to dive into their business problems and every-body gets a chance to give feedback. The space has felt so safe to me, and these people have now become my friends. I would highly recommend Six Figure Dinners. It's been really great for my business and for my own mental state as a Founder," said Lydia Davis, CEO of the Teemates App. Time and time again, I hear the same thing from other members. Why so?

Six Figure Dinners stands as a distinctive and exclusive peer advisory group, designed to cater to the needs of small business owners with annual revenues ranging from $500K to $5 million. At its core, Six Figure Dinners is a dynamic meeting platform where CEOs and entrepreneurs come together to engage in the art of knowledge sharing and mutual growth acceleration. It's a place where the power of collective wisdom is harnessed, fostering a unique and enriching experience for its members.

Central to the Six Figure Dinners experience are the monthly dinner meetings, an opportunity for these driven business leaders to gather in an intimate and collegial setting. These gatherings offer a haven for candid discussions, insightful conversations, and the exchange of real-world experiences. It's a place where challenges are met with solutions, and where members empower one another through their collective expertise.

Imagine spending several hours each month with peers whom you can be honest with, both in terms of sharing your challenges and celebrating your victories. This is exactly what sets Six Figure Dinners apart. The presence of a board of advisors, a team of seasoned experts ready to offer personalized coaching and tailored guidance to each member, provides a wealth of strategic insights, enabling business owners to make informed decisions and navigate the intricate landscapes of entrepreneurship with confidence.

Additionally, Six Figure Dinners opens the doors to a vast network of expert consultants spanning various fields, creating an invaluable resource for members seeking specialized knowledge and solutions. These connections, coupled with the genuine camaraderie that emerges from the group's intimate and engaging environment, serve as catalysts for meaningful relationships and enduring collaborations.

Six Figure Dinners is not just a group; it's a testament to the power of collaboration, knowledge exchange, and collective growth, designed to help entrepreneurs navigate complexity and drive sustainable growth in their businesses. It's also a testament to the power of well-managed meetings, as I implement all of my successful management strategies. Before each meeting, I create and deliver an agenda clarifying the purpose. My meetings are predictable in terms of the timeline and timeframe for each individual's participation. And I do my best to manage the dynamics in a thoughtful, yet empowering manner. Everything I've learned about meetings and how to run them is deployed at Six Figure Dinners.

Why Six Figure Dinners?

Entrepreneurs and business owners often find themselves perched at the summit of their organizations, which might look prestigious, but it can also be remarkably isolating. The relentless pursuit of their goals and the constant decision-making can take a toll. This sentiment isn't reserved only for entrepreneurs; it's a shared experience among many in leadership roles. The responsibilities and pressures they shoulder can leave little time for nurturing relationships outside their professional lives. It's enough to drive anyone to the brink.

Entrepreneurs often face significant uncertainty and risk as they invest time, money, and effort into their ventures. The risk and associated fear of failure, and the financial and emotional consequences that come with it, can lead to anxiety and stress. Entrepreneurship often requires long working hours and a high level of dedication. The constant pressure to perform and meet deadlines can lead to burnout and exhaustion, which are risk factors for mental health issues. Financial instability and the need to secure funding or manage cash flow can also be a source of stress for many entrepreneurs. Financial worries can take a real toll on mental well-being for everyone, but especially when it is felt for staff and vendors as well.

On top of all of this, entrepreneurship can be a lonely endeavor, especially in the early stages of a startup when the entrepreneur may be working alone or with a small team. Combined with an unhealthy work-life balance, which can lead to stress, strained relationships, and a neglect of personal well-being, it can truly be a "lonely at the top" experience.

I personally experienced these challenges when I founded and operated my own start-up. After receiving my MBA from the UCLA Anderson School of Management, where I also worked at Goldman Sachs and Rosewood Capital, I launched into the food-service industry. In less than a few years, I co-owned and operated eleven frozen yogurt shops and a food truck in the Houston, Texas, area. It was the most exhilarating and demanding time of my life. But did I love every minute of it? Not by a longshot.

Being an entrepreneur often comes with the feeling of loneliness at the top. The journey of building and leading a business can be isolating because the decisions and responsibilities ultimately rest on your shoulders. The weight of making tough choices, managing risks, and charting the course for your venture can be overwhelming. As the leader, you may also find it challenging to confide in or seek advice from others within your organization, leading to a sense of solitude. It's during these moments that the support of a trusted network, mentors, or fellow entrepreneurs can be invaluable, providing not only guidance but also a sense of camaraderie that helps combat the loneliness that can accompany the entrepreneurial path.

The truth is, at the time, I probably did have people to talk to. But as is so common among entrepreneurs and leaders, I isolated myself. The isolation led to a dearth of honest communication and feedback. In my case, it resulted in some bad decision making, despite being surrounded by people who wanted to help. I simply refused to listen, but only because I was trapped in a situation I allowed myself to be in. I dug my own hole, so to speak.

Indeed, many entrepreneurs and business owners are surrounded by employees and advisors who may hesitate to voice their concerns or criticisms openly. This absence of candid dialogue can hinder growth and innovation, as constructive feedback and diverse perspectives are essential for making informed decisions and overcoming obstacles. Breaking free from this isolation and fostering a culture of open communication is a vital step in not only alleviating the loneliness at the top but also in propelling businesses toward greater success.

This is why I created Six Figure Dinners. Over time, the interactions and discussions within Six Figure Dinners led to the development of meaningful relationships among members. Entrepreneurship can be a lonely journey, but these relationships provide a sense of belonging and support that extend beyond the business realm. It empowers participants to stop digging their own hole and climb out of it. It's a time and place where leaders can be honest with each other.

When people finally feel safe, in a meeting environment that is controlled and encourages authentic participation, they begin to value their own private "board of advisors" who've navigated the very challenges they are facing. But it's not just about receiving; it's also about giving back. Our community thrives on mutual support, where every member is eager to lend a hand. You're not just getting advice; you're also joining a circle of trustworthy peers—a collective brain trust where every question is met with diverse perspectives, ensuring you always have the best possible path forward.

I invite you to visit our website at SixFigureDinners. com to learn more.